PLATED DINOSAURS

KU-655-738

W
FRANKLIN WATTS
LONDON•SYDNEY

Franklin Watts
This edition published in the UK in 2017 by The Watts Publishing Group

Copyright © 2013 David West Children's Books

All rights reserved.

Designed and illustrated by David West

ISBN: 978 1 4451 5508 1

Printed in Malaysia

Franklin Watts
An imprint of
Hachette Children's Group
Part of The Watts Publishing Group
Carmelite House
50 Victoria Embankment
London EC4Y 0DZ

An Hachette UK Company.
www.hachette.co.uk

www.franklinwatts.co.uk

PROFESSOR PETE'S PREHISTORIC ANIMALS PLATED DINOSAURS
was produced for Franklin Watts by
David West Children's Books, 6 Princeton Court, 55 Felsham Road, London SW15 1AZ

Professor Pete says:
This little guy will tell you something more about the animal.

Learn what this animal ate.

Where and when (Mya=Millions of Years Ago) did it live?

Its size is revealed!

How fast or slow was it?

Discover the meaning of its name.

A timeline on page 24 shows you the dates of the different periods in Mya.

Contents

Crichtonsaurus was a plant eater.

 Crichtonsaurus means 'Crichton's lizard' after Michael Crichton, the author of *Jurassic Park*.

 It lived in China during the Lower Cretaceous period, 95–90 Mya.

 Crichtonsaurus grew up to 3 metres in length and weighed 0.9 tonnes.

 Crichtonsaurus had a slow walk that reached a speed of 9 kilometres per hour.

Professor Pete says:
Although it had plates like a Stegosaurus, Crichtonsaurus was more closely related to Ankylosaurus.

Crichtonsaurus

CRY-ton-sore-us

This armoured dinosaur had a strange collection of bony nodules along its back. Some stood upright to form small plates like those of a Stegosaurus.

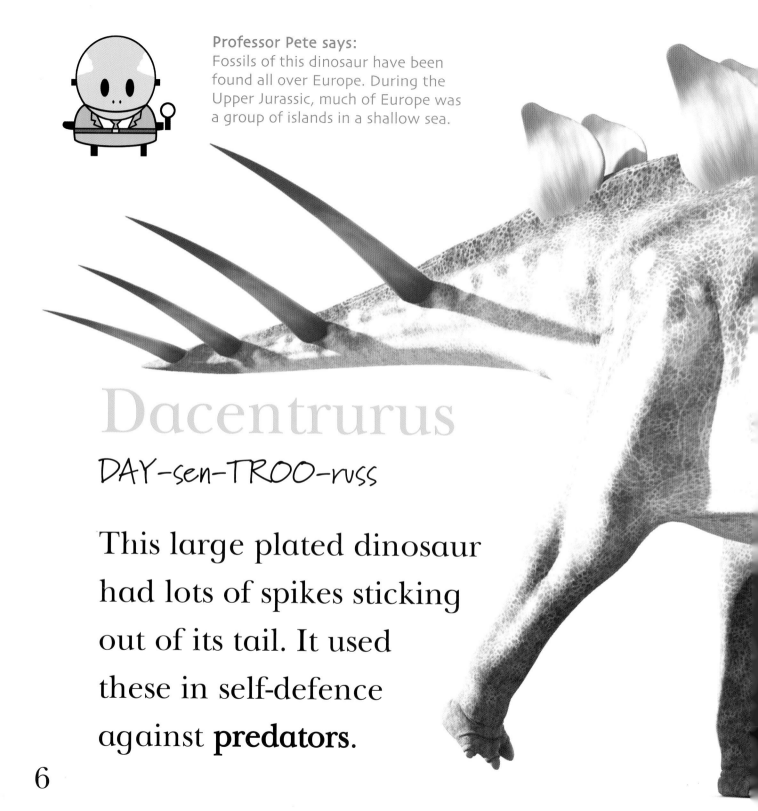

Dacentrurus

DAY-sen-TROO-russ

This large plated dinosaur had lots of spikes sticking out of its tail. It used these in self-defence against **predators**.

6

Dacentrurus was a plant eater.

Dacentrurus had a maximum speed of around 9 kilometres per hour.

Dacentrurus means 'very pointy tail'.

It lived in England, France, Portugal and Spain during the Upper Jurassic period, 154–150 Mya.

Dacentrurus grew to 6 metres in length and weighed 1.8 tonnes.

Gigantspinosaurus

GEE-gant-SPINE-oh-sore-us

This small plated dinosaur had a
large curved spike sticking
out sideways from
its shoulders.

Professor Pete says:
The plates on the back of
Gigantspinosaurus were
small compared with other
plated dinosaurs.

Gigantspinosaurus was a plant eater. It probably ate low-lying vegetation.

Gigantspinosaurus wasn't very fast. It could probably reach 7 kilometres per hour.

Gigantspinosaurus grew up to 4.2 metres long and weighed 700 kilogrammes.

It lived in China during the Middle Triassic period, 160 Mya.

Gigantspinosaurus means 'giant spined lizard'.

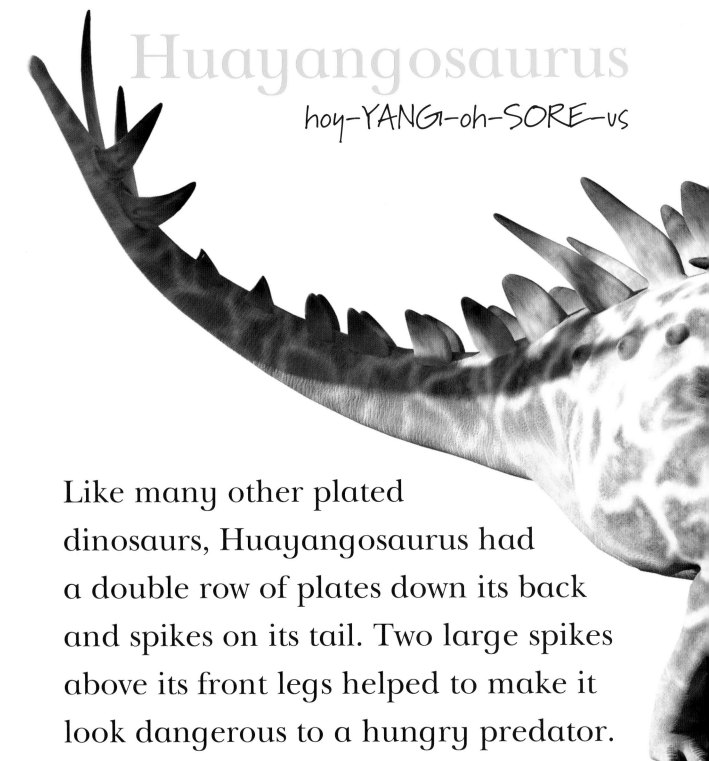

Huayangosaurus

Like many other plated
dinosaurs, Huayangosaurus had
a double row of plates down its back
and spikes on its tail. Two large spikes
above its front legs helped to make it
look dangerous to a hungry predator.

10

Huayangosaurus was a plant eater. It probably ate low-lying vegetation.

 Huayangosaurus could probably reach 7 kilometres per hour.

 Huayangosaurus grew up to 3.7 metres long and weighed 227 kilogrammes.

 It lived in China during the Middle Triassic period, 165 Mya.

 Huayangosaurus means 'Huayang lizard', named after the province where it was discovered.

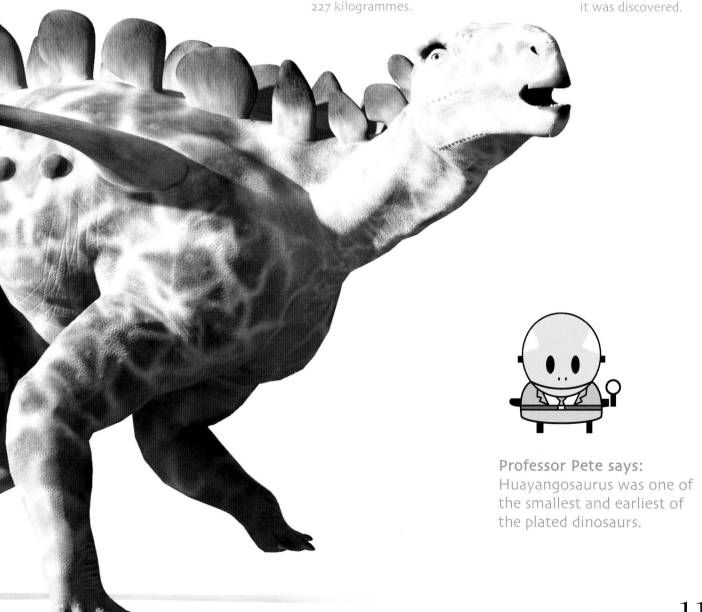

Professor Pete says:
Huayangosaurus was one of the smallest and earliest of the plated dinosaurs.

Kentrosaurus

ken-TROH-sore-us

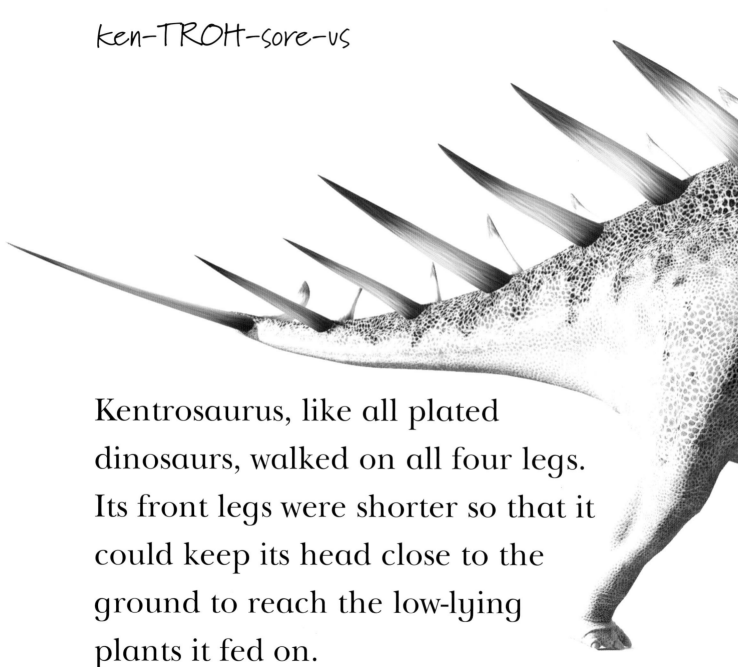

Kentrosaurus, like all plated dinosaurs, walked on all four legs. Its front legs were shorter so that it could keep its head close to the ground to reach the low-lying plants it fed on.

Kentrosaurus was a plant eater.

Kentrosaurus means 'spiked lizard'.

Kentrosaurus grew up to 4.5 metres in length and weighed 1.4 tonnes.

It lived in Tanzania during the Upper Jurassic period, 155–150 Mya.

Kentrosaurus could probably reach 9 kilometres per hour.

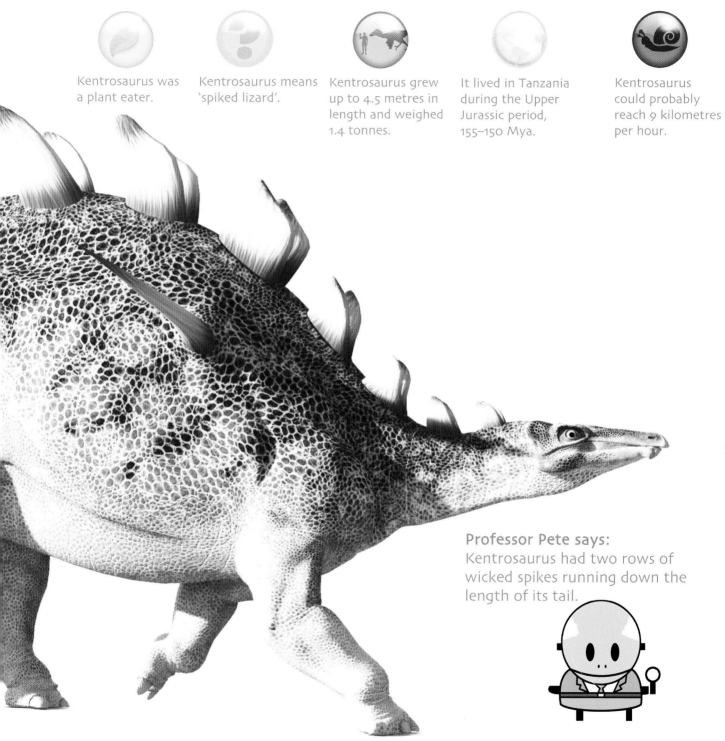

Professor Pete says:
Kentrosaurus had two rows of wicked spikes running down the length of its tail.

13

Lexovisaurus

lex-OH-vee-sore-us

Similar to Kentrosaurus, this spiky, plated dinosaur had two rows of small plates and large spikes. It also had spikes protruding from its shoulders. Its tail ended in a set of spikes called a thagomizer.

Professor Pete says:
The word thagomizer comes from a cartoonist. **Paleontologists** liked the word and decided to use it.

Lexovisaurus grew up to 19.7 metres in length and weighed around 2 tonnes.

It lived in England and France during the Middle Jurassic period, 170–150 Mya.

Lexovisaurus means 'Lexovii lizard', named after an ancient tribe from Europe.

Lexovisaurus was a plant eater, browsing on ferns and **cycads**.

Lexovisaurus could probably manage 9 kilometres per hour.

15

Miragaia grew up to 6.1 metres in length and weighed around 0.9 tonnes.

Miragaia moved on four legs and was not a fast runner.

It lived in Portugal during the Upper Jurassic period, 150 Mya.

Miragaia is named after the area in Portugal where its fossils were found.

Miragaia was a plant eater.

Professor Pete says:
Scientists think its long neck allowed it to feed on higher vegetation than other dinosaurs. This meant it did not compete with them for food.

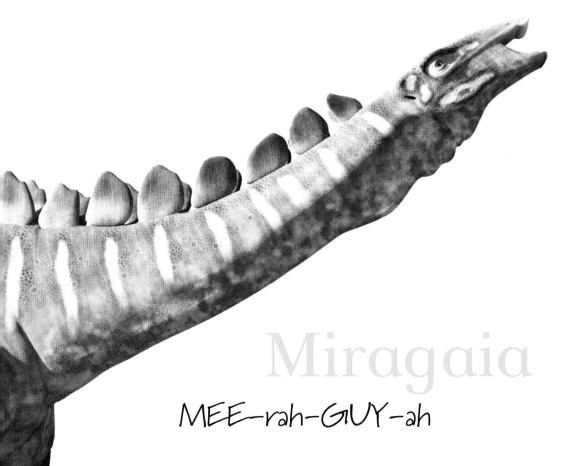

Miragaia

MEE-rah-GUY-ah

Miragaia was an unusual-looking plated dinosaur. It had a long neck that made it look like a **sauropod**. It had a double row of small plates that ran from its head to its tail. It had a thagomizer and small side spikes.

Stegosaurus

STEG-oh-sore-us

The large plates on Stegosaurus's back may have contained blood vessels. Scientists think they could have helped control its body temperature just like a car's radiator.

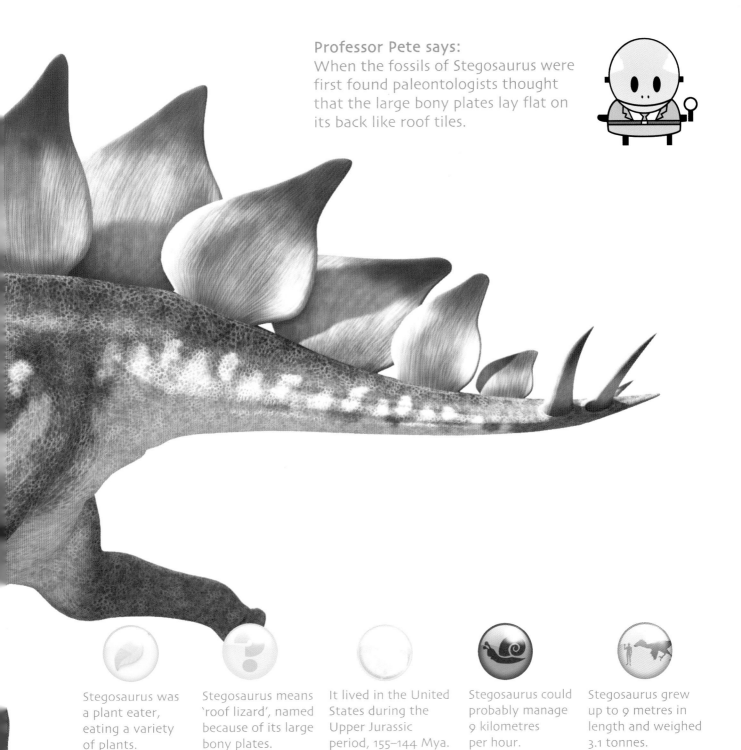

Professor Pete says:
When the fossils of Stegosaurus were first found paleontologists thought that the large bony plates lay flat on its back like roof tiles.

Stegosaurus was a plant eater, eating a variety of plants.

Stegosaurus means 'roof lizard', named because of its large bony plates.

It lived in the United States during the Upper Jurassic period, 155–144 Mya.

Stegosaurus could probably manage 9 kilometres per hour.

Stegosaurus grew up to 9 metres in length and weighed 3.1 tonnes.

Tuojiangosaurus

too-YANG-oh-sore-us

Tuojiangosaurus had a similar layout to most plated dinosaurs. The plates on its back, though, were thinner.

Like Kentrosaurus it had a large spike sticking out sideways from its shoulder.

Tuojiangosaurus ate plants.

Tuojiangosaurus means 'Tuo River lizard'.

Tuojiangosaurus was 7 metres long and 2.7 tonnes in weight.

Tuojiangosaurus was not able to run very fast.

It lived in China during the Upper Jurassic period, 157–154 Mya.

Professor Pete says:
The spines and plates that can be seen on plated dinosaurs were not attached to the skeleton. They grew out from the skin.

Wuerhosaurus ate plants.

Wuerhosaurus lived in China during the Lower Cretaceous period, 137–99 Mya.

Wuerhosaurus means 'Wuerho lizard' from where its fossils were found in China.

Wuerhosaurus may not have been able to run fast, but it could spin quickly to hit its attacker with its thagomizer!

It measured up to 8 metres in length, and up to 2 tonnes in weight.

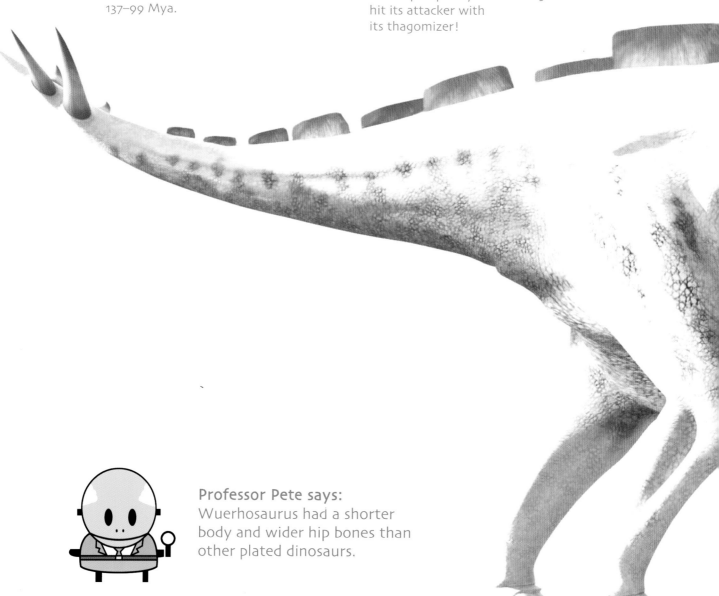

Professor Pete says:
Wuerhosaurus had a shorter body and wider hip bones than other plated dinosaurs.

Wuerhosaurus

woo-uhr-huh-sore-us

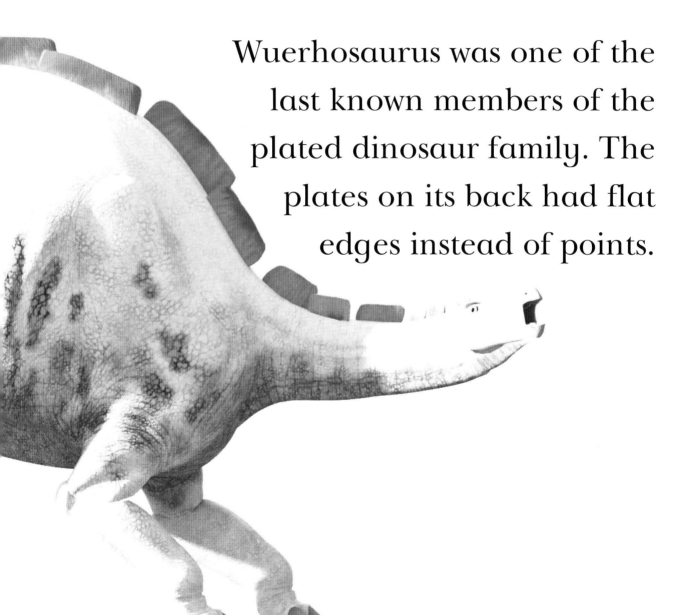

Wuerhosaurus was one of the last known members of the plated dinosaur family. The plates on its back had flat edges instead of points.

Glossary

cycads
Palm-like plants.

paleontologist
A scientist who studies early forms of life, chiefly by studying fossils.

predators
Animals that hunt and kill other animals for food.

sauropod
A family of dinosaurs with long necks and long tails such as Diplodocus.

Timeline

Dinosaurs lived during the Mesozoic Era which is divided into three main periods.

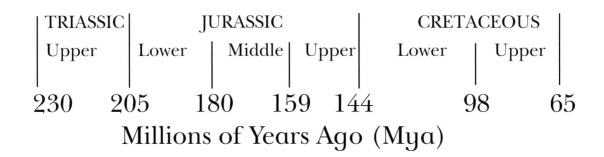

TRIASSIC	JURASSIC			CRETACEOUS	
Upper	Lower	Middle	Upper	Lower	Upper
230	205	180	159	144	98	65

Millions of Years Ago (Mya)